Christian Strassburger

Financing in life sciences biotech companies

Dokument Nr. V70419 aus dem GRIN Verlagsprogramm

Christian Strassburger

Financing in life sciences biotech companies

GRIN Verlag

Bibliografische Information der Deutschen Nationalbibliothek: Die Deutsche Bibliothek verzeichnet diese Publikation in der Deutschen Nationalbibliografie; detaillierte bibliografische Daten sind im Internet über http://dnb.d-nb.de/ abrufbar.

1. Auflage 2006

http://www.grin.com/
Druck und Bindung: Books on Demand GmbH, Norderstedt Germany
ISBN 978-3-638-90343-1

PFORZHEIM UNIVERSITY

School of Design, School of Engineering,

and Business School

Programme

Master of Arts in International Finance and Accounting

WS 2006/07

Financing in Life Sciences
Biotech Companies

Christian Straßburger

Date of Submission: 30. November 2006

Content

Table of Figures

1 Introduction

Biotechnology is a more and more important field of research in present. Publicly we are currently confronted with many questions about the rights and wrongs within this field of science, like how to handle the issue of gene manipulation or stem cell research. However, biotechnology is more than just an accumulation of ethical questions and science – it is a whole industry and as such interesting for investors.

The scope of this paper is not dealing with the topics discussed in glossy magazines, but it addresses the issues of corporate finance in biotechnology. In order to get an overview of the industry from a finance point of view, the industry has to be portrayed. Hence, this is the topic of chapter two.

From the point of the investors, and therefore of the capital markets, the understandability of the segment biotechnology, and thus the availability of crucial information has to be ensured.

Consequently the transparency of the biotechnology segment and of the individual enterprises, respectively, are the topics of the third chapter. The implications of this chapter have a strong impact on the valuation of biotechnological companies and the sector as a whole – a subject dealt with in chapter number four.

The fifth chapter is concerned with the core topic of this paper and identifies and analyses different sources of finance for biotechnology enterprises. Thereby it is taking the point of view of the biotechnology firms and the potential investors. The paper is showing important difficulties and advantages connected with the different approaches. Additionally the chapter also describes and evaluates the risks of different options of investors.

The paper is concluded with a summary of the findings in chapter six showing that investing into biotechnology is worth thinking about for a responsible and sophisticated investor, although the segment is a difficult field incurring many risks, however opportunities for the "big win", as well.

2 Life Science – An Overview

As there is no fundamental definition of what life sciences includes, however most of the institutions adapted the definition of the OECD - Organization for Economic Cooperation and Development – that consists of two more or less consistent parts. The OECD offers a deliberately broad definition:

> *"The application of science and technology to living organisms, as well as parts, products and models thereof, to alter living or non-living materials for the production of knowledge, goods and services."*[1]

However, the OECD points out that a more specified explanation of the definition used should be given. The second part of the OECD definition lists therefore the activities it sums up under its definition of biotechnology:[2]

- **DNA/RNA:** Genomics, pharmacogenomics, gene probes, genetic engineering, DNA/RNA sequencing/synthesis/amplification, gene expression profiling, and use of antisense technology.
- **Proteins and other molecules:** Sequencing/synthesis/engineering of proteins and peptides (including large molecule hormones); improved delivery methods for large molecule drugs; proteomics, protein isolation and purification, signaling, identification of cell receptors.
- **Cell and tissue culture and engineering:** Cell/tissue culture, tissue engineering (including tissue scaffolds and biomedical engineering), cellular fusion, vaccine/immune stimulants, embryo manipulation.
- **Process biotechnology techniques:** Fermentation using bioreactors, bioprocessing, bioleaching, biopulping, biobleaching, biodesulphurisation, bioremediation, biofiltration and phytoremediation.
- **Gene and RNA vectors:** Gene therapy, viral vectors.
- **Bioinformatics:** Construction of databases on genomes, protein sequences; modelling complex biological processes, including systems biology.
- **Nanobiotechnology:** Applies the tools and processes of nano/microfabrication to build devices for studying biosystems and applications in drug delivery, diagnostics etc.

Nevertheless, the capital markets understand under Life Sciences the fields Biotechnology, Pharmaceuticals, Pharmaceutical Technology, and Health Care. The differentiation of Red, Green and White Biotechnology is another distinction that is made in modern biotechnologies.

---

1 OECD (2006), p. 1.
2 OECD (2006), p. 1.

2.1 Red, Green and White Life Science – What is the difference?

The color differentiation within the life sciences is mainly based upon the prevailing application. However, aspects such as the acceptance by the population, the importance of the market, its maturity and its growth potential are also considered.

The red biotechnology deals with the matters of human and beast health and therefore receives a high acceptance in the population.[3] This toleration is also due to the fact, that new and innovative medications have been developed for treatments of formerly incurable diseases. The dominating driver of innovation in this field is the biotechnology that is also the main driver of the pharmaceutical industry – an industry currently under pressure due to the expiration of many patents. Most of the biotechnology businesses traded on stock exchanges are situated in the red segment of biotechnology.[4]

The green biotechnology is concerned with agricultural and food development and is currently struggling with consumer's acceptance. Especially in Europe and above all in Germany "Gen-food"[5] is disapproved. Most of the activities in this sector are integrated in the activities of large groups, e.g. BASF, Bayer, Monsanto, Syngenta.[6]

The use of biotechnological methods in the industrial production, as well as environmentally save production processes, environmental protection and redevelopment are part of the white biotechnology. However, its use in specific processes are rather difficult to identify for investors without profound knowledge of the processes within a business.

The focus of this paper is the red biotechnology due to its attractiveness for investors. The importance for the pharmaceutical industry that incurs high growth potential, as well as a generally high acceptance, is the foundation of the strong interest of the capital markets in the red biotechnology.

2.2 Current Trends in the Biotech Segment

The current situation of western societies is the predominant driver in biotechnology, especially the demographic challenges have a strong impact on the growing recognition of

[3] Cp. DVFA e.V. (2005), p. 2.
[4] Cp. DVFA e.V. (2005), p. 2.
[5] Genetically modified food is regularly in the news.
[6] Cp. DVFA e.V. (2005), p. 3.

the biotechnology sector. Particularly in Germany the demographic structure is transforming from a pyramid form in the 1950s towards a mushroom form in the near future.[7] The ageing population is the reason and the source of the current and future potential that is seen in biotechnology.[8] As there is only therapy for one third of all known diseases, new therapies that are based upon biotechnological substances may offer innovative treatments. Furthermore the traditional diseases that are associated to ageing, such as rheumatism, diabetes and cancer represent a high potential and are in the focus of many biotechnological R&D projects.[9]

Molecular diagnosis is another interesting field in modern biotechnology. It represents a possibility to diagnose bacterial and viral infections and is applied to identify hepatitis and HIV germs in stored units of blood.[10] Other imaginable applications are certainly considering new treatments for influenza viruses and related diseases like SARS. These new diagnostic applications imply an enormous growth potential for the biotechnology segment and related industries such as the pharmaceutical industry that provides the preparation kits for subsequent analysis.[11]

Many of the big pharmaceutical companies are currently very eager in investing in biotechnology, because the patents for their blockbuster products are expiring or expire in the near future. This has crucial implications for their sales and their turnover, as cheaper imitations will float the market immediately.[12] Thus the new biotechnological medications are a welcome new business line that is both unique and (currently) hard to copy. Additionally to the investments in a wide range of biotechnological activities and supporting technologies that cover the whole value chain[13], the pharmaceutical companies are anxious to acquire niche products in order to diversify on the one hand and to be a first mover in an upcoming market on the other one.[14]

[7] Cp. Statistisches Bundesamt (2003), Graph 2003-15-0220.
[8] Cp. DVFA e.V. (2005), p. 5.
[9] Cp. DVFA e.V. (2005), p. 6.
[10] Cp. DVFA e.V. (2005), p. 8f.
[11] Cp. DVFA e.V. (2005), p. 9.
[12] E.g. Ratiopharm in Germany.
[13] Cp. DVFA e.V. (2005), p. 20, 21.
[14] Cp. DVFA e.V. (2005), p. 22.

Another crucial factor for newcomers in the market are the new regulations by officials, such as the new department of the FDA[15] for post market surveillance of new medications.[16] However, the improved terms of contract for partnerships, licensing agreements and cooperation are also a strong incentive for start-ups in this market.[17]

All of the above mentioned effects, especially the commercial interest of the big pharmaceutical companies, are increasing the value of the whole biotechnology segment and improve the financing possibilities for new companies.

2.3 Business Models in Biotech

The businesses in the biotechnological segment are characterized by their activities and may be differentiated accordingly. The different business models do have distinguishable cash flows, risk profiles, and growth and business potential.[18] However the classification seems difficult, as the enterprises constantly adopt to the market circumstances. Furthermore the market is in constantly changing.

The pharmaceutical development companies are goal oriented and try to develop new products to cure known diseases or to reduce handicaps caused by diseases. There might be a differentiation according to presence in the value chain. A fully integrated biotechnological enterprise is present at all steps of the value chain and produces a turnover by selling its products.[19]

The companies that offer molecular diagnostic instruments may be differentiated from the pharmaceutical developers as there are viewer and less strict official licensing regulations, shorter development cycles and therefore lower development costs.

The technology and service providing enterprises are subordinate within the whole value chain. However, they have a strong impact on the sector as they provide technologies that increase productivity in production and R&D.[20] Often such enterprises own patents for their technologies and lease them to third parties.

15 US American Food and Drug Administration
16 Cp. DVFA e.V. (2005), p. 17.
17 Cp. DVFA e.V. (2005), p. 19.
18 Cp. DVFA e.V. (2005), p. 22.
19 Cp. DVFA e.V. (2005), p. 22.
20 DVFA e.V. (2005), p. 23.

Moreover, research indicated that most business models have also and "extended"[21] version. Additionally to the core competency consideration stated above, these versions try to include other important measures, such as financing, product and market development, return mechanisms and resources.[22] Therefore many of those versions exist and it would exceed the scope of this paper to examine all of them.

[21] DVFA e.V. (2005), p. 24.
[22] Cp. DVFA e.V. (2005), p. 24.

3 Transparency in the Biotechnology Sector

Fundamentally the transparency of businesses financed by the capital market needs to be rather good in order to gain the trust of investors. Therefore the information concerning products, activities, financial results and strategies have to be communicated in a clear and effective way. The official rules and regulations are a set of minimum standards. The importance of different investor relations instruments is to bee seen in Figure 1.[23]

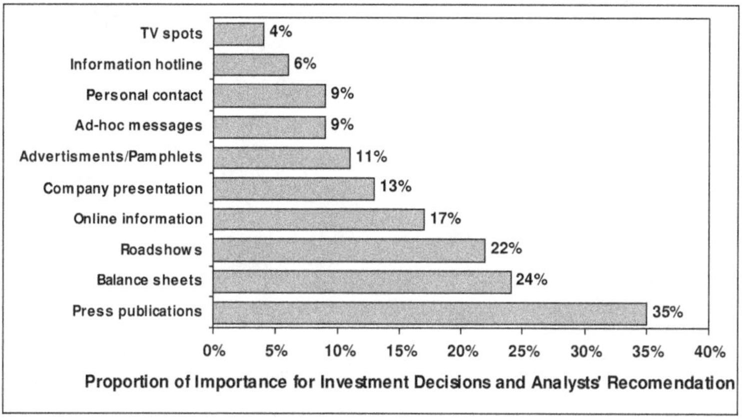

Figure 1: Importance of IR Activities for Investment Decisions and Analysts' Recommendations (Source: DVFA (2005), p. 32).

A professional investor relations management is beneficial especially for the biotechnology businesses as most of them are not yet profitable and are evaluated according to their future potential to generate profits.[24]

3.1 Specifics in Investor Relations

Due to the fact that biotechnology businesses do usually not generate enough profits to cover their costs, a steady and reliable information is therefore requested by investors. Instruments that play a major roll in the biotechnological segment are: press conferences, individual conversations with major investors, participation in branch conferences, R&D

[23] DVFA e.V. (2005), p. 32.
[24] Cp. DVFA e.V. (2005), p. 28f.

days, biotechnology forums, phone conferences concerning publications, as well as any other form of information events.[25]

Concerning press conferences the issue for biotechnology businesses is not only to inform the general public and the investors about the current implication, but certainly analysts. Especially when major strategic decision have been made, such as acquisitions, discontinuance of a product line or the sale of a division, analysts might not only be interested about current, but about the mid and long term implication.[26] Therefore many biotechnology enterprises organize a special conference for analysts at least once a year, where the future effects of the decision on potential future cash flows and the value of the company are discussed, background information may be distributed and questions concerning the rationales behind decisions may be answered.[27]

Some analysts play an even more important roll. Big investors and many important groups of investors employ their own analysts which have to be considered opinion formers and multipliers. Therefore it is often crucial to keep a good relationship to those analysts and organize a fluent information flow, often more detailed and complex in nature than the general publications. This process is managed by a IR-Manager that is also the person to turn to for "One-on-One-Meetings"[28], on which usually a member of the board is present as well. Due to the multiplier function of these crucial analysts the whole capital marked benefits from this special relationship.[29]

3.2 Specifics in Corporate Governance

Corporate Governance – the management and revision structure of an enterprise with a management board, a supervisory board and a general meeting – is gaining importance under the aspect of transparency. Since 2002 there is a legal standard in Germany (TransPuG + KonTraG in 2005) that supports the corporate governance idea of national and international investors.[30]

Major elements of the corporate governance codex are the independent supervisory boar, an adequate remuneration of the management in comparison to the sector, an adequate

[25] Cp. DVFA e.V. (2005), p. 27.
[26] Cp. DVFA e.V. (2005), p. 33.
[27] Cp. DVFA e.V. (2005), p. 33.
[28] DVFA e.V. (2005), p. 33.
[29] Cp. DVFA e.V. (2005), p. 34
[30] Cp. DVFA e.V. (2005), p.36. see also: www.corperate-governance-code.de

proportion of personal liability of the management for careless actions, the quality of share option remuneration in order to increase lasting employer-employee relationships, and the compliance with accounting regulations.[31]

3.3 Specifics in Financial Accounting and Reporting

All biotechnological enterprises have to comply with their national GAAP. However, to attract international investors many companies also publish their financial statements according to US-GAAP or IFRS.[32] In Germany this is even required by law for companies oriented to the financial markets since 2005 (4. Dec. 2004), however there is an extension of two years period for companies using US-GAAP. [33]

[31] Cp. DVFA e.V. (2005), p.36f.
[32] Cp. DVFA e.V. (2005), p. 37
[33] Cp. BilReG, Artikel 10, 4.12.2004.

Regardless whether the companies us national GAAP, e.g. German HGB, or IFRS, they do face the problem that the standards have been created for traditional and profitable companies. Therefore their information content concerning a biotechnological enterprise is rather deficient. This is a result of the business model that is based upon long initial research periods where no profits are generated. Part of this problem is, that all investments in R&D are accounted for on the cost side, meaning that non of the medications and other new biotechnological products that are being developed are assets in a balance sheet. Even though under IFRS it is possible to capitalize[34] immaterial assets, there is the restriction to do this only if a commercialization is probable. For all other R&D projects the capitalization is, however, still forbidden. The picture that is created by a financial statement according to these regulations does not reflect the true and fair view on a biotechnological company as it neglects the value drivers in this industry – namely the research and development. This is a disadvantage for both investors and enterprises seeking financial sources.

[34] Translation of the German word: aktivieren. Gräfer/Scheld (2005), p. 664.

4 Company and Sector Valuation

Even if a biotechnology start up is complying with all requirements of transparency, the valuation of such an enterprise is difficult. Particularly for investors the valuation is a crucial factor when they determine the structure of their investment portfolio. However, especially in the biotechnology segment company and sector valuation must consider certain specifics explained in this chapter.

4.1 Valuation Approaches

In the biotechnology segment a traditional approach to evaluate a company is of very little use for numerous reasons: very complex business models, specific success factors and risk profiles, and the particular valuation of the product pipeline.[35] The use of traditional DCF-approaches is sub-optimal considering the negative cash flows to be expected over a not yet determined period. Similar, the use of peer-group benchmarking might not be sufficient due to the various specializations of the individual biotechnology enterprises.

It turns out that a method- mixture combining traditional approaches as DCF and peer-group benchmarking complemented with qualified analyst opinions concerning the quality of information given to investors is the most practical approach.[36] Furthermore, the economic environment has to be taken into consideration using a sector valuation by Porter's five-forces model.

4.2 Five-Forces Model for the Sector

The most common approach to evaluate a business segment is the five-forces model developed by M. Porter in 1972. The model considers five fundamental factors that should be further subdivided into determinants crucial for the enterprise and the segment. Figure 7 (Appendix) provides a brief overview for the biotechnology segment.[37]

Using the analysis, the enterprise's comparative strategy is to be evaluated it the segment's context. This evaluation might use the SWOT concept and classify the enterprise into a category of a portfolio analysis tool, such as the BCG or McKinsey matrix.

[35] Cp. DVFA e.V. (2005), p.46.
[36] Cp. DVFA e.V. (2005), p.46.
[37] Cp. DVFA e.V. (2005), p. 50f

4.3 Traditional Valuation and Specifics for Biotech

In most cases the quantitative evaluation concepts oriented towards the capital markets are not of much use, as the biotechnology enterprises are in the beginning usually not listed. Therefore, orientations such as the price-earnings ratio or the enterprise value by market capitalization do not exist.[38] The use of traditional fundamental analysis approaches as the DCF method are similarly displeasing as there is much risk involved in the future development of the enterprise. The use of a Monte Carlo simulation takes some of the risk factors into consideration, however it's use is time and money consuming and therefore rare. Furthermore the use of multipliers as indicated with the peer group valuation seems to be difficult as one of the characteristic of biotechnology enterprises is that they develop treatments that are supposed to be unique.[39]

Concerning the qualitative evaluation methods, only half of the aspects in focus have some value for the evaluation of a biotechnology enterprise. Aspects, such as the structure of shareholders, the financial structure, the plausibility and the adaptability of the business model and the risk management, have been developed for traditional businesses in the production segment. They are rather useless when it comes down to evaluate an innovative new business. However, the aspects attractiveness of the segment, investor relations/corporate governance, quality of management, partnerships, patents, and structure of the enterprise may give some reasonable valuation orientations.[40]

As mentioned before, to come to a fair valuation their has to be a mixture of traditional and sector specific methods. The above mentioned traditional valuation methods are one part of this mix, but due to the scope of this paper are not examined any further. However, the mixture of these methods led to the development of a Biotechnology Discount Model by certain banks.[41] Some criteria of these Biotechnology Discount Models are worth mentioning here.

At first, the models are based upon a discounted future cash flow of the first two or three years of profitability. Furthermore the tax rate is supposed to be normalized and differed losses are ignored. The profits are not risk adjusted, but represent a best case scenario, e.g.

38 Cp. DVFA e.V. (2005), p. 54.
39 Cp. DVFA e.V. (2005), p. 54.
40 Cp. DVFA e.V. (2005), p. 56-66.
41 E.g. Bank Vontobel, Morgan Stanley, UBS. Cp. DVFA e.V. (2005), p. 68.

a medication is in clinical phase III is assumed to get to market for sure (even though only 60 to 80 % of the medications reaching clinical phase III actually are getting to market). [42]

In the second phase of the model, the Price-Earnings ratio is predicted for the second or third year of profitability, and multiplied with the best-case-scenario profit prognoses for the same year.[43] As comparison "blue chip" enterprises in the current biotechnology market are taken.

The established market capitalization is then discounted considering individual risks, such as development risks, regulatory risks, and marketing risks.[44] The value determined is the current value of the enterprise.

Even though the model is almost exclusively used in the American market, it might become popular in Europe, as well, when more and more biotechnology enterprises become profitable and participate in the capital markets.[45]

However the model must be criticized. Especially the fact, that only the best case scenario is taken into consideration and the assumptions of future development and growth is strongly unrealistic. Furthermore, the determination of the discount factor is not transparent at all, but depends rather on the assumptions of few (maybe well qualified) individual analysts and does not reflect a true market opinion.

After describing the specific model to evaluate a biotechnology enterprise, it is however not surprising that there are even more detailed specifics to be considered for pharmaceutical companies and technology/service providers, respectively.

4.4 Specifics for Pharmaceutical Development

The main driver of pharmaceutical developers is of course the product pipeline. Therefore this aspect of the business model calls for an intensified recognition to quantify the value of a specific pipeline. In the following, the basic approaches underlying various evaluation models are to be described.

Translating the peer group comparison used in company valuation is called the pipeline comparable approach.[46] This method categorizes the different medication developments

[42] Cp. DVFA e.V. (2005), p. 68.
[43] Cp. DVFA e.V. (2005), p. 68.
[44] Cp. DVFA e.V. (2005), p. 69.
[45] Cp. DVFA e.V. (2005), p. 69.

according to their clinical phase and compares the structure of the pipeline with the known values of pipelines with the same structure. This approach is simple, however it does not recognize the specifics of the medication developments, development risks, or profit potentials.[47] Furthermore, it is based on historic experience rather than future expectations.

The real option pricing approach is an approach evaluating different decision alternatives in each clinical phase and using the option pricing model (Black-Scholes Formula) to evaluate a pipeline. However, the often insufficient data available and the difficult modeling method often prevent the sufficient use of this method.[48]

Finally the use of the risk adjusted present value of the pipeline, is often the foundation of evaluation models. These models do not account for risks by using a single discount factor, but rather adjusts the expected future cash flows according to the success potential of their underlying product developments.[49]

4.5 Specifics for Technology- / Service- Providers

The valuation of a technology or service provider in the biotechnology segment is even less standardized than in the field of pharmaceuticals. However, the DVFA Life Science Commission considers the following qualitative aspects especially important: leading or monopoly position and attractiveness of the technology, degree and intensity of innovation, client structure, market entry barriers, relative turnover development.

The leading position and the attractiveness of the technology is considering the uniqueness of the technological solution and the competitive advantage the enterprise therefore has. However the judgment of these factors is quite difficult. Hence, further subdivision of considerable factors is to be done. Those factors are: the kind of technology that is used, the maturity of the enterprise and the technology or service, the potential to create further innovation of the technology, the compatibility of the technology with other technologies and its substitution risks, the acceptance of the technology by clients and consumers, and the potential use of the technology in other unrelated fields.[50]

[46] Cp. DVFA e.V. (2005), p. 69.
[47] Cp. DVFA e.V. (2005), p. 69.
[48] Cp. DVFA e.V. (2005), p. 69.
[49] Cp. DVFA e.V. (2005), p. 69.
[50] Cp. DVFA e.V. (2005), p. 87.

Additionally, marketing is one of the focal points when considering the degree and intensity of innovation a business is able to create. With innovation the advantages a new service or technology offers to customers is described. The issue focuses usually on one of the following improvements: cost savings, time savings, fewer failures, higher quality or quantity (including e.g. reaching a never before met goal), more security, or new before unknown applications.[51] The degree of innovation describes, how strong the advantage is for the customers; the intensity of innovation evaluates the capability of an enterprise to continue to create innovations.

When looking at the client structure the client's nature and quality are issues to be evaluated. The goal is to evaluate the economic reliability of the clients and to draw a conclusion from there to the client's future demands and liquidity. What is more, the client's nature may have implications for the degree of innovation of the enterprise and might contain risks and opportunities for the marketing of innovations.[52]

Patents are the most significant market entry barriers in the biotechnology segment. However, faster development and speedier market introduction and penetration, cost advantages due to economies of scale, established standards, product families ("One stop shop") and branding are as well important entry barriers.[53]

The relative turnover development is the ratio of the enterprise's turnover considering the average market growth and the development of competitors. This evaluation aspect has to consider furthermore the growth of the enterprise – that might be organic or based upon M&A activities.[54]

The overall picture of the analysis exposed above may be finalized in a SWOT analysis or using a Scorecard approach. A comprehensive documentation and explanation of the methods used and the assumptions made has to be provided to the sophisticated person using the evaluation analysis for investment decisions in order to ensure transparency.[55]

[51] Cp. DVFA e.V. (2005), p. 87f.
[52] Cp. DVFA e.V. (2005), p. 89.
[53] Cp. DVFA e.V. (2005), p. 90.
[54] Cp. DVFA e.V. (2005), p. 91.
[55] Cp. DVFA e.V. (2005), p. 92.

5 Financing Sources

The financial sourcing of a biotechnology enterprise is the most crucial issue for the industry. The reason for the difficulties most of the biotechnology start ups have with financing is the very nature of their business – that is the research on new innovative drugs, cures, methods and processes and for its innovative nature containing numerous risks for the investors.

According to a study of Ernst & Young (2005) the sources of capital for German biotechnology enterprises are mainly institutional and public/governmental investors. Other sources of finance, including private and strategic investments, accumulate to only one third of the source for capital (see also Figure 8, Appendix).

However, the sector is starting to grow independently. As the study indicates, almost one third of all German biotechnology enterprises is able to source its financial needs completely out of its turnover.[56] Furthermore, the small number of listed companies (only 6 %[57]) is surprising in an international context. The portion of companies that are financed by Venture Capital is 62 % in the German market. [58] This portion includes not only initial investments, but also subsequent (later stage) investments.[59] Nonetheless, the proportion of enterprises that used a third stage investment increased (from 24% in 2003 to 27% in 2004)[60], also due to the lack of new biotechnology enterprises to enter the VC market. On the other hand do many biotechnology companies (1/3 of all) expect to generate profits in the next three years, of those about 40% are currently financed by venture capital.

The equity of the biotechnology segment again increased in 2004 to about 548 million Euro, which is about 150 % of the year ahead. However it does not reach the high peak in 2000(1,4 billion Euro).

5.1 Initial Financial Sourcing

As the introduction of this chapter already indicated there are different sources of finance for biotechnology enterprises. Almost most important are the public sources of finance –

56 Cp. E&Y(2005), p. 103.
57 E&Y(2005), p. 103.
58 E&Y(2005), p. 103.
59 Cp. E&Y(2005), p. 103.
60 E&Y(2005), p. 103.

governmental support programs. Nonetheless, the most important source of finance are Venture Capitalists. Currently less important, however in the future probably becoming much more significant, are private investors. The strategic investments represent the last distinguishable source of finance that will be examined in the following.

5.1.1 Governmental Funds and Politics

Characteristical for Germany is the strong relevance of the banking sector when sourcing investment capital. This fact has crucial implications on the financing possibilities of start ups in biotechnology, because German banks and insurance companies represent quiet conservative and risk-averse investors. Additionally the findings of Kulicke (1993) show that the founders of biotechnology start ups are more often not experienced in market oriented economics and marketing than it is the case in other industries. Biotechnology start ups need more management support than the start ups of other segments, e.g. Engineering.

Therefore the German government identified different aspects to start support programmes, namely: foundation of new biotechnological funds, support of existing investmenttrusts[61] and capital suppliers with: a governmental hedge of the defaults during the first few years of the investment, subsidies or low interest loans for biotechnology enterprises that are bound to an investmenttrust, and limited subsidies for the expenses of investmenttrusts due to the involvement with a biotechnology start up.[62]

In 2001 the German government proclaimed the research investment programme "Biotechnologie" that complemented an initiative started in 1999 and the fund for the national human genom project (DM 350 million) with additional DM 1.5 billion.[63] This initiative was embedded into the framework biotechnology[64] that finally amounted to EUR 802.7 million for the period 2001 to 2005.[65] In 2006 the German government announced the following initiative - "The High-Tech Strategy for Germany". The programme is supposed to offer Euro 15 billion for top technologies (the proportion for biotechnology amounting to Euro 430 million) for the period 2006 – 2009.[66] This amount (Euro15 bil.) is

61 Translation of the German term: Beteiligungsgesellschaft, Fremdwörterbuch Duden.
62 Reis/Koschatzky (1997), p.93.
63 BMBF (7/2001).
64 „Rahmenprogramm Biotechnologie –Chancen nutzen und gestalten", BMBF (4/2001).
65 Cp. BMBF (4/2001), p.42.
66 Cp. BMBF (2006), p. 7.

to be increased to three percent of the GDP of Germany in 2010. However the programme refers to the federal states and communities as major governmental source of finance for the top technologies (adding to about Euro 260 billion p.a.).[67] The German government passed on the responsibility to administer and manage the sponsored projects mainly to other institutions, most important of all the "Jülich Forschungszentrum".[68] Moreover the BMBF also offers an web portal to hand in applications for research projects.[69]

However, the DIB – German Association of Biotechnology Industries – has some suggestions to further improve the financing situation of biotechnology start ups. These suggestions basically concern tax issues that are quiet specific in Germany. The first suggestion is to exclude the use of § 8 Abs. 4 KStG for Venture Capital financing and later IPO. This paragraph deals with the losses carried forward that are not to be used when an enterprise is changing its legal form or more than 50 % of the nominal capital is added to the current capital.[70] This is a crucial issue for fast growing enterprises due to the high capital requirements during the period between the start up and the initial marketing campaign. The second suggestion is concerned with the income tax. The DIB demands an increase of the tax free stock amount from currently 1% (material stake) of the business's stocks to 10% or Euro 500,000, respectively.[71] Furthermore the time limit of tax free sale of the stocks under the material limit shall be reduced from 5 years to 2 years. [72] This change would encourage especially private investors that are only investing small amounts to invest more into start ups as their shares would be better marketable. Furthermore the reduction of the tax free sale period is supposed to increase the market for these shares and therefore improve the market of biotechnology shares. The third suggestion of the DIB is a new treatment of non-marketable stock options that are used for employee remuneration. Currently they are taxed under graduated income tax and the value is assumed to be the difference of the advertised price and the market value of the option. The sale of the shares is treated according to the individual income tax. The DIB now demands a treatment of the shares sold after opting according to the specific German partial exemption method

67 Cp. BMBF (2006a), p. 13.
68 BMBF (2006b).
69 See: http://foerderportal.bund.de/.
70 DIB (2006), p.3f.
71 DIB (2006), p.4.
72 DIB (2006), p.4.

(Halbeinkünfteverfahren).[73] This would increase the value of a stock option for the employees and therefore further ease the financial situation of start ups.

5.1.2 Incubation Concept

Another very important governmental support is the incubation concept that is applied on the federal state and the community level. The incubation concept basically tries to support young enterprises that lack a resource allocation due to market inefficiencies.[74] Biotechnology is one of the sectors that is especially affected by such inefficiencies.[75] This is due to the nature of the cash flows generated by a biotechnology start up as described in chapter 4. The incubation concept is offering:[76]

1. advisory services through the incubator management,
2. networking capacities due to the closeness to other start ups and to established companies, and
3. cost savings due to reduced administrative and transaction costs, as well as lower rents and subscription fares due to shared research and information service use.

Furthermore, incubators often offer financial support, further education (e.g. in economics and marketing), and public relations support.

The concept is a transition of the medical incubator used to ensure the survival of premature infants in a controlled environment.[77] In Germany the first "Technology and Founders Center" was opened in Berlin in 1983 by the ADT e.V. It has about 168 members and supports about 7,500 enterprises.[78] Incubation conceptions may be classified into five categories having different initiators and target groups:

	Support-oriented Incubators	Research-oriented Incubators	Profit-oriented Incubators	Strategic Incubators	Hybrid Incubators
Initiator	States, Communities, Non-Profit-Organizations	Universities	Venture Capitalists, Business Angels	Enterprises	Conglomerates of initiators with different motivations

[73] DIB (2006), p.5.
[74] Cp. Proff (2000), p. 150.
[75] Cp. Böhringer/Bukowsky/Maurer (2005), p. 319.
[76] Cp. Böhringer/Bukowsky/Maurer (2005), p. 321.
[77] Cp. Böhringer/Bukowsky/Maurer (2005), p. 320.
[78] ADT-Bundesverband e.V. (2006), p. 1.

Motive	Politics, Job Creation, Structural sub-sidies, Basic Re-search, Economic Growth	Educational Policy, Trans-lation of Theory into Praxis, Re-search activities	Profit from value increase of the shares in the start ups, e.g. at IPO	Penetration of future markets, Basic research, Acquisition of new customers, Profit	Depends on the combination of initiators
Target group	Regional start-ups	High-Tech Start-ups, often University Spin-offs	High-Tech Start-ups with high capital requirements	Spin-off, Spin-in	Combinations

Figure 2: Forms of the Incubation Concept (Source:Böhringer/Bukowsky/Maurer (2005), p. 322).

However, as the incubation conception tries to protect the start ups from the unfavorable environment, there are certain risks for the supporters and for the start ups as well.[79] Due to the fact that the scarcity of resources on the market is partially eliminated, developing companies may tend to inappropriate generosity when handling their resources. Furthermore, especially new incubators may not meet the needs of their participants due to a single-sided portfolio strategy of the supporter. Another risk for the start ups may be the monopoly position of the incubator to acquire certain information or the access to networks and partners. Incubators often have an impact on the start up enterprise's reputation even after their establishment in the market. Hence, the choice of the right incubator may have a crucial impact on the midterm development of a company. Last, but not less important, is the effect the incubator may have on the independence of the decision making of a new enterprise. Since the incubator offers a lot of support, the phase after this support is canceled is crucial.[80]

"Incubation concept" is barely used in today's every day language. The terms center or park describe, however, the same approach. Examples in Germany are: Biotechnologiepark Luckenwalde, Biotechnologiepark Köln, Biotechnologiezentrum Bremerhafen, Biotechnologiezentrum Münster, etc..

[79] Cp. Böhringer/Bukowsky/Maurer (2005), p.325f.
[80] Cp. Böhringer/Bukowsky/Maurer (2005), p.325f.

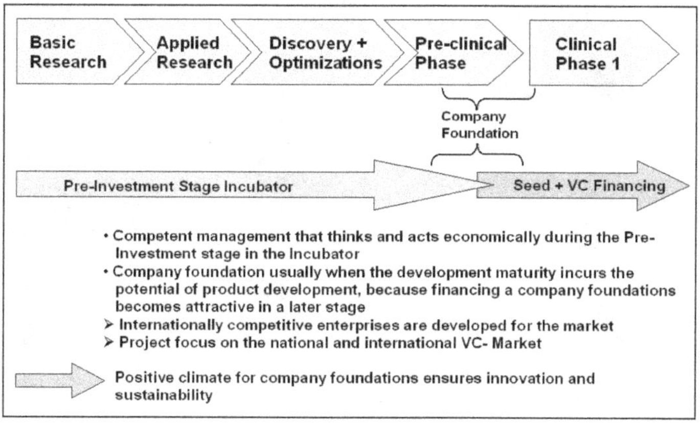

Figure 3: Incubation Concept concerning the Pre-Investment Stage of Biotechnology (Source: Domdey (2006), p. 124).

The German government is also a supporter of this approach and finances excellent projects within incubation concepts with Euro 150 mil. each year in six slides. The program, called GO-Bio, focuses thereby on Pre-Seed-Incubation meaning especially basic research that will lead to profitable products in a longer (than the venture capital) time horizon (see Figure 3).[81]

5.1.3 Private Equity

The use of private equity is another alternative for financing a biotechnology enterprise. However, the term might be misleading because it describes the whole market for capital used as equity:[82]

> "Private equity provides equity capital to enterprises not quoted on a stock market. Private equity can be used to develop new products and technologies, to expand working capital, to make acquisitions, or to strengthen a company's balance sheet. It can also resolve ownership and management issues. A succession in family-owned companies, or the buyout and buyin of a business by experienced managers may be achieved using private equity funding. Venture capital is, strictly speaking, a subset of private equity and refers to equity investments made for the launch, early development, or expansion of a business."

[81] Cp. Domdey (2006), p. 124-126.
[82] Cp. Weiding/Mathonet (2004), p. 6.

That definition includes venture capital as being just a certain form of private equity, just like buyouts and mezzanine capital.[83] However, sometimes a differentiation of private equity and venture capital is made depending rather on the maturity of the investment object. Venture capital is usually referred to as risk capital and therefore is used in the start up phase of an enterprise, also called a seed finance and early growth finance.[84] Private equity investments are less risk taking and therefore only available for enterprises with a certain maturity.[85] Furthermore are private equity investors – often institutional investors – looking for established companies that they may acquire for a low price, and which they can sell later on with a profit. They buy enterprises in order to restructure, to dispose incidental assets, and to improve operations and management.[86] Furthermore using a Leveraged-Buy-Out financing they squeeze out profits of the company while holding it.[87]

A venture capital financing might be reclassified according to this definition, when an enterprise is going into the marketing phase with one or several new products – becomes a later stage venture, respectively.[88] The risk profile changes for the investor as well as for the company owners and therefore the sources of finance and the numbers of investors willing to take the residual risks multiply.

5.1.4 Venture Capital

Venture Capital (VC), often also referred to as risk capital, has been the most important source of finance for German biotechnology companies in during the last decade – up to 2003 it has actually been the only source, except for governmental programs. The total amount of venture capital in the biotechnology segment realized a growth rate of an average of 5 % (not including the boom years 2000 and 2001).[89]

Usually biotechnology start ups are not able to acquire enough finance to do the necessary investments into their research and development capacities out of their revenues. Venture Capitalists offer the necessary financial muscles to get the researchers ideas into a marketable product. Therefore they usually acquire a large amount of the start up providing

83 Cp. E&Y(2005), p. 111.
84 Cp. Ross/Westfield/Jordan (2006), p. 500.
85 Cp. E&Y(2005), p. 111.
86 Cp. Brealy/Myers (2000), p.990.
87 Cp. Brealy/Myers (2000), p.990.
88 Cp. Prose (1998), p. 25.
89 E&Y(2005), p. 105.

equity to the enterprise and getting a share in the company in return.[90] However, to convince a Venture Capitalist to join a biotechnology enterprise, the founders have to fulfill certain criteria. A necessary prerequisite is a profound business plan. Venture Capitalists may demand seats in the board of directors of the start up enterprise demanding not only a certain control, but also offering expertise concerning judgment of contracts. The investment of the founders' (and managers' and researchers') private fortunes into the start up signals to Venture Capitalists their faith in the business.[91] It also creates a very strong commitment of the involved persons to their project which in turn is taken positively into consideration by Venture Capitalists. Furthermore Venture Capitalists usually collaterise their investment by choosing a model consisting of preferable shares that convert into ordinary shares in case of profitability and into super senior liabilities in case of a failure.[92]

Even if Venture Capitalists believe in the business idea of a biotechnology start up, they usually do not give the full amount necessary to develop a marketable product at once. Instead they split their investment according to certain financing stages, already mentioned in the introduction to this chapter. This encourages constantly high commitment to the development projects and limits the losses in case of an early failure. This risk reducing strategy is due to the fact, that only two out of 10 venture capital financed enterprises survive successfully and end up as self-sufficient enterprise. Statistically however, only one will pay off big.

5.1.5 Business Angles

The question of who is actually willing to invest in a high risk company reveals the terms Business Angles or Family Offices that appear in the press from time to time.[93] The terms are used to describe the investments in Private Equity (PE) financing of start up companies done by wealthy individuals or families. They usually believe in the business idea of the founders and support them with expertise in financing, management, strategy, human resources, and a less strong focus on the performance.[94] This form of financing is giving the start up the chance to concentrate on its core idea, which might be a competitive

90 Brealey/Myers (2000), p.406.
91 Leland/Pyle (1977), p.371ff.
92 Brealey/Myers (2000), p.407.
93 Cp. Schmidt Brand (2006), p.140f; Klernent (2006), p.1; The Herald (2006), p. 5.
94 Cp. Weidig/Mathonet (2004), p. 8.

advantage, rather than dealing with the divergent issues of its investors.[95] This form of financing has already become a standard vehicle for biotechnology enterprises in the USA to raise funds.[96]

However, the most important fund for biotechnology enterprises are the Venture Capital Funds that aim at taking the companies public as soon as they have a marketable product in order to cash in.[97] During the last few years the frequency of large IPOs has yet decreased, compared with the boom years of 2000 and 2001 dramatically decrease, which might be a thread to the financing opportunities of biotechnology firms.[98]

5.1.6 Strategic Investments and Other Financing Possibilities

Besides investment companies and funds, other corporates may be a source of finance. Examples for strategic investments may be the support of Cellzome and MorphoSys by Novartis.[99] These strategic investments might also be an exit strategy for the initial capital providers, an issue to be discussed in the next section of this chapter. Furthermore are corporations also supporters of incubators as mentioned earlier in this chapter.

However, there are more possibilities for biotechnology enterprises to finance. The possibility to finance partially through mezzanine capital and to issue convertibles are already common approaches in the US biotechnology segment.[100]

5.2 Secondary Financial Sourcing

After the initial capital from the investors, companies often face financial distress due to capital need for clinical phase tests, marketing campaigns, or for the set-up of production facilities. The capital markets might be source of finance as examples form Australia show.[101] However, the issuance of additional shares after a biotechnology enterprise has concluded an IPO is tricky, as shareholders might disapprove. Therefore, companies in the USA started to issue restricted stock awards supported by warrants, which might however

95 Cp. Schmidt-Brand (2006), p. 141.
96 Cp. Hochwimmer (2006), p. 192.
97 Cp. Hochwimmer (2006), p. 192.
98 Cp. Hochwimmer (2006), p. 192.
99 Cp. E&Y (2005), p. 111.
100 Cp. Hochwimmer (2006), p 191.
101 Cp. Schmidt-Brand (2006), p. 141.

interfere with German law.[102] Another possibility is the issuance of convertible bonds or debentures.

In Europe the most interesting stock markets for biotechnology enterprises seem to be the AIM London, however the Frankfurt stock exchange with its Entry Standard is also an option worth taking into consideration.[103] The fund raising on the capital markets is a very important brick in the financial structure of a biotechnology enterprise after leaving the initial start up phase.[104] However, some funds do participate in second and third round financing as well.

5.3 Investor's Strategies

After looking at the point of the biotechnology company, it is interesting what the possibilities of investors are. As it has been explained broadly, the investment into a start up biotechnology enterprise is a risky investment. However such risks may be substantially reduced using different investment strategies, as the findings of Weidig and Mathonet (2004) of the European Investment Fund show. Unfortunately these findings are not exclusively focused on biotechnology, but they certainly have implications on this growth segment as well. From an investor's point of view there are four vehicles to a private equity investment: direct investment, funds, fund-of-funds, and more exotic products like collateralized fund obligations.[105]

5.3.1 Direct investments

This category of equity investment is the most work intense one for investors as they have to provide not only capital, but additional management support as already explained earlier in this chapter (see Venture Capital and Business Angles).

The difficulty of a direct investment is also the company valuation that depends on possible entry and exit prices, as well as the offer and demand for shares in such a company. The specifics in evaluating a biotechnology enterprise and the incurred risks have already been discussed in chapter four. However, to better point out the risk of a

[102] Cp. Hochwimmer (2006); p. 192.
[103] Cp. Hochwimmer (2006), p.190.
[104] Cp. Hochwimmer (2006), p.190.
[105] Cp. Weidig/Mathonet (2004), p. 6.

direct investment the probability of getting a return from the investment in terms of multiples of this investment is presented in the following figure:

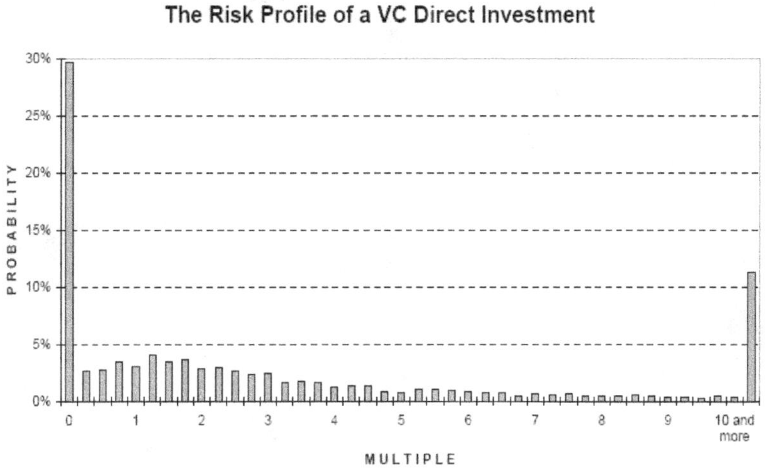

Figure 4: The Risk Profile of a US Venture Capital Direct Investment (Source: Cochrane (2003)).

As the graph shows about 30% of all VC investments are total losses, and about 42 % do not get to the break even point. The implication for investors must be:[106]

1. If the business is perfectly understood, and the selection skills ensure a "sure bet"[107], commit all capital to only one direct investment (and crack the jackpot).
2. If the selection skills are superior, but not quiet 100%, conduct several diversified investments.
3. If the selection skills are not sufficient, do not invest directly.

5.3.2 Private Equity Funds

The investment into private equity might be carried out via funds indirectly, a system where a fund collects capital from investors to choose and manage about 10 to 20 direct investments on their behalf.[108] As it has been explained in chapter 5.1.1 , the German investment market is dominated by banks, pension funds and insurers. It is not surprising, that these institutions also are the main capital providers (limited partners) of private equity funds: banks 25%, pension funds 25%, insurers 10%, corporate investors 10% and

[106] Cp. Wedig/Mathonet (2004), p. 9.
[107] Cp. Wedig/Mathonet (2004), p. 9.
[108] Cp. Wedig/Mathonet (2004), p. 12.

others.[109] The costs of the set up of the fund managing partnership and the management fees amount to usually 3.5% of the drawn capital, and additionally to about 20% of the generated returns for the fund's management (general partner) due to their commitment to the companies and their expertise in reducing risks.[110] As Figure 5 shows, the risks of a venture capital fund in Europe is distributed quiet symmetric, and virtually excludes total losses:

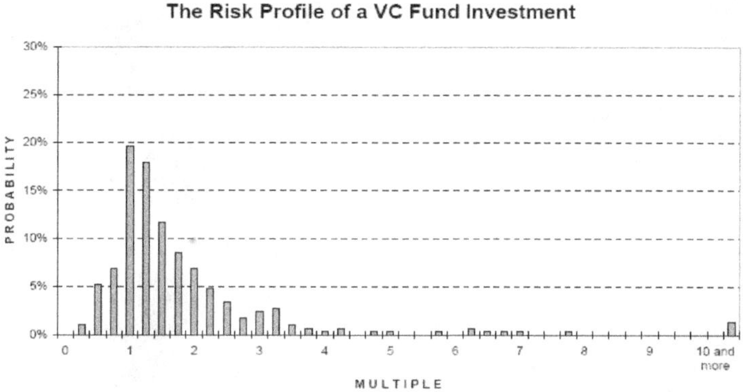

Figure 5:The Risk Profile of European Venture Capital Funds (Source: Weidig/Mathonet (2004), p. 14).

The investment into a fund induces significant diversification effects, however there are still losses for about 30% of the investments, and the possibility of a big win is considerably reduced compared to a direct investment. Moreover, specific knowledge about a business sector such as biotechnology is not necessary. Instead the knowledge of the fund managers and their expertise are the value drivers.

5.3.3 Fund-of-Funds

A fund-of-funds collect capital from investors to invest into 20 or more funds on their behalf making it easy for the investors to invest and to diversify on a global basis. Investors are characteristically pension funds, banks, insurance companies, corporate investors, and other funds-of-funds.[111] The portion of finance raised by funds-of-funds has been increasing over the last few years and accumulates to about 10% (2004) of all private

[109] Cp. Wedig/Mathonet (2004), p. 12.
[110] Cp. Wedig/Mathonet (2004), p. 12.
[111] Cp. Wedig/Mathonet (2004), p. 16.

equity investments.[112] The management of a fund-of-funds charge about 0.5% of the raised capital management fee and additionally 5 to 10% profit participation.

As the risk profile of Figure 6 shows, the risk is quiet symmetric distributed and does not pronounce any total losses. Furthermore, Weidig and Mathonet mention the similarity to an efficient market portfolio.[113] This form of investment is clearly the least risky from an investor's point of view. The knowledge about the fund's management is again the value driver in this kind of transaction.

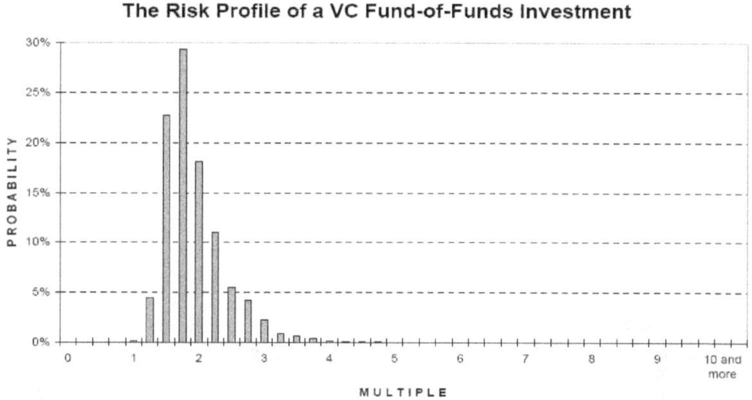

Figure 6:The Risk Profile of European VC funds-of-funds (Source: Weidig/Mathonet (2004), p. 17).

5.3.4 Comparison of Risk Profiles

Comparing the risk profiles just explained, one comes to the conclusion, that a direct investment is most risky, however incurs the possibility for a big win. The diversification effect reducing the risk when investing into a fund or fund-of-funds is clearly observable (see comparison in Figure 9, Appendix).

5.3.5 Alternative Investment Vehicles

There are still more opportunities for investors to place their money in the private equity market that are worth mentioning.

[112] Cp. Wedig/Mathonet (2004), p. 12.
[113] Cp. Wedig/Mathonet (2004), p. 16

Most important of all is probably the Collateralized Fund Obligation (CFO) used mainly to secure private equity funds.[114] This vehicle has gained importance over the last decade and consisted often of convertible notes or bonds. The main aim is to adapt the risk to the investor's profile in order to raise capital or sell off the underlying equity portfolio.[115]

Another vehicle are the publicly traded private equity products (PTPE) that raise capital from the financial markets and reinvest into private equity. PTPE is often classified into three groups: listed companies with the core business in private equity (e.g.3m), quoted investment funds (e.g. Schroeder Ventures Trust), and specially structured investment vehicles (e.g. Castle Private Equity).[116]

Furthermore there are so called secondary funds that buy limited partnership shares of funds or secondary directs, and venture-leasing funds that lease equipment in exchange for equity.[117]

5.4 Exit Options for Initial Capital Providers

Exit strategies are the options that capital providers have in order to get back their initial investment. In Germany the preferred option to sell the share or investment in the biotechnology enterprise has been and still is the Trade Sale and the IPO.[118] An exit is however only possible when the research has been successful and the outcome is a promising potential for a future blockbuster product generating a yearly turnover of at least USD 1 billion.[119] It is not unusual that such promising inventions have been the fruit of co-operations an that a partner of the pharmaceutical industry is the participant of a license agreement or a trade sale (sale of the shares to a buyer with a strategic motivation – usually acting in the same business sector). Such partnerships are especially useful when it comes to the preparation of the clinical test phases, due to its costs. The counter move is either a license agreement as just mentioned, or a full sale of the marketing right.[120]

If the option of going public is appreciable, most companies – almost one third of those participating in an E&Y biotechnology study for 2004 – would decide for the Frankfurt

[114] Cp. Wedig/Mathonet (2004), p. 25.
[115] Cp. Wedig/Mathonet (2004), p. 25.
[116] Cp. Wedig/Mathonet (2004), p. 25
[117] Cp. Wedig/Mathonet (2004), p. 27; and Cp. Harvard Biotechnology Club (2006), p1.
[118] Cp. E&Y (2005), p. 98.
[119] Cp. Büchter/Nastos (2006), p. 138.
[120] Cp. Büchter/Nastos (2006), p. 138.

Stock Exchange (FWB). The second position in this ranking is represented by the Swiss Sock Exchange (SWX) and the third position is hold by the US Exchange NASDAQ.[121]

For both mentioned exit strategies a valuation of the company and its product pipeline is necessary. The difficulties and specialties of an evaluation of a biotechnology enterprise have been discussed in chapter 4.

[121] Cp. E&Y (2005), p. 98.

6 Summary

As the analysis of the biotechnology segment has clearly carved out, this industry is not easy to understand and its participants have to be quiet sophisticated in order to participate in its science, as well as in its finance.

The different fields of biotechnology have to be separately examined due to the different parameters that influence their dynamics which have been examined in the second chapter. These differences have certain implications on the development and the business models applicable. Furthermore the complexity of the whole industry stresses the need of efficient information flows from the enterprises to investors, which is summarized under the term transparency in chapter three.

For investors and the financial markets, that are sources of finance, the valuation of a company is given priority. However, besides the traditional valuation approaches that are only partially of use, the biotechnology segment demands special treatments in order to take all aspects of this innovation driven industry into consideration. Chapter four has illustrate the different valuation approaches and it is concluded that the rather simple valuation approaches in combination of the trust in analyst with in depth industry knowledge is the right approach for evaluating a biotechnology enterprise.

Due to the above mentioned difficulties of assessing biotechnology, especially in innovative scientific fields, the sourcing of finance is a difficult task for start up enterprises. The sources of finance for such new companies are examined in the first part of chapter fife (5.1 and 5.2), followed by a brief description of the secondary sources of finance. Furthermore, the second part of chapter five (5.3 and 5.4) takes the point of view of investors, hence evaluates the attractiveness of different investment options according to the incurred risks.

Summarizing the paper, it is clear that biotechnology is not a field for average entrepreneurs or investors. Both parties have to have a deep understanding of the underlying scientific methods, approaches and goals in order to evaluate their feasibility. Furthermore a mutual support has to be agreed upon in order to ensure the success of the project. However, still there is a high risk of failure that might, from an investor's point of view, be eliminated using diversification of certain investment instruments. For the biotechnology entrepreneur there seem to be few opportunities to reduce their risk. Finally,

an investment in biotechnology might be an option for sophisticated investors and for the general public that uses such individuals to act on their behalf. There is much risk incurred on the one hand, but the possibility for extraordinary large returns on the other hand.

Sources

ADT-Bundesverband e.V. (2006): Netzwerk deutscher Innovationszentren, URL: www.adt-online.de, date, 11.11.06.

BMBF (4/2001): Rahmenprogramm Biotechnologie –Chancen nutzen und gestalten, Bonn.

BMBF (7/2001): Bundesministerium für Bildung und Forschung, Pressemitteilung 7/2001.

BMBF (2006a): The High-Tech Strategy for Germany, Berlin/Bonn.

BMBF (2006b): Biotechnologie, URL: http://www.bmbf.de/_search/searchresult.php?URL=http%3A%2F%2Fwww.bmbf.de%2Fde%2F1024.php&QUERY=biotechnologie, date: 11.11.06.

Böhringer, A.E.O./Bukowsky, I./Maurer, I. (2005): Das Inkubatorkonzept als Chance für den Gründungserfolg: Handlungsempfehlungen für junge Hochtechnologie-Unternehmen, in: BfuP 57 (2005), Heft 4, p. 319-332.

Brealey, R.A. /Myers, S.C. (2000): Principles of Corporate Finance, 6th ed., inter alia Boston/New York/San Francisco.

Büchter, S./Nastots, A. (2006): Finanzierung von Geschäftsmodellen im Bereich Biopharmaka, in: GoingPublic Sonderausgabe "Biotechnologie 2006", Wolfratshausen, p. 138-139.

Cochrane, J. (2003): The Risk and Return of Venture Capital, NBER Working Paper series, WP8066,

DIB (2006): Beseitigung steuerrechtlicher Hemmnisse für das nachhaltige Wachstum neu gegründeter Biotechnologie und anderer Hightech-Unternehmen, Frankfurt.

Domdey, H. (2006): Von der Forschung zur Innovation. Neue Förderstrategie des BMBF, in: GoingPublic Sonderausgabe "Biotechnologie 2006", Wolfratshausen, p. 124-125.

DVFA e.V (2005): Life Science am Kapitalmarkt, Biotechnologie im Focus, Dreieich.

Ernst & Young (2005): Deutscher Biotechnologie-Bericht 2005, Mannheim.

Gräfer,H./Scheld, G.A.(2005): Grundzüge der Konzernrechnungslegung, 9th ed, Bamberg.

Harvard Biotechnology Club (2006): Start up Plan, URL: http://www.thebiotechclub.org/industry/startup/resources_ventlease.php, date: 26.11.2006.

Hochwimmer, G. (2006): Biotech-Finanzierung in Nordamerika. Schwingt das Pendel nach Europa?, in: GoingPublic Sonderausgabe "Biotechnologie 2006", Wolfratshausen, p. 190-193.

Klernent, A. (2006): Business Angel im Interview – Der Himmel hellt sich auf, in: Die Zukunftsmacher, n-tv, URL: http://www.n-tv.de/725567.html, date: 26.10.2006.

Kulicke, M (1993): Chancen und Risiken junger Technologieunternehmen. Ergebnisse des Modellversuchs „Förderung technologieorientierter Unternehmensgründung" (TOU). Heidelberg. (Technik, Wirtschaft und Politik Schriftreihe des Frauenhofer-Instituts für Systemtechnik und Innovationsforschung, Bd. 4)

OECD (2006): Statistical Definition of Biotechnology, Statistical Definition of Biotechnology (UPDATED IN 2005), URL: http://www.oecd.org/document/42/0,2340,en_2649_37437_1933994_1_1_1_37437,00.html, Visited: 25. 10. 2006. Proff, H. (2000): Möglichkeiten einer effizienten Förderung von Technologie- und Gründerzentren – Eine wirtschaftspolitische Analyse, in: Jahrbuch für Regionalwissenschaft, Vol. 20, S. 149-179.

Prose, S.D. (1998): The Economics of the Private Equity Market, ECONOMIC REVIEW THIRD QUARTER 1998, FEDERAL RESERVE BANK OF DALLAS, p. 20-34.

Ross/Westfield/Jordan (2006): Corporate Finance Fundamentals, 7th ed, inter alia Boston/London/San Francisco.

Schmidt-Brand, J. (2006): Alternative Finanzierungsformen für junge Biotech-Firmen, in: GoingPublic Sonderausgabe "Biotechnologie 2006", Wolfratshausen, p. 140-141.

Statistisches Bundesamt (2003): Entwicklung der Altersstruktur in Deutschland 1959 - $2050_{estimated}$, Graph 2003-15-0220..

The Herald (2006): no author, Three up for financial Challenge, in: The Herald – Web issue 2682, November 20, 2006, URL: http://www.theherald.co.uk/business/74817.html, date: 20.11.2006

Weidig, T./Mathonet, P-Y. (2004): The Risk of Private Equity. Private equity is a risky asset, but private equity investments are not secessarily so, Luxembourg.

Appendix

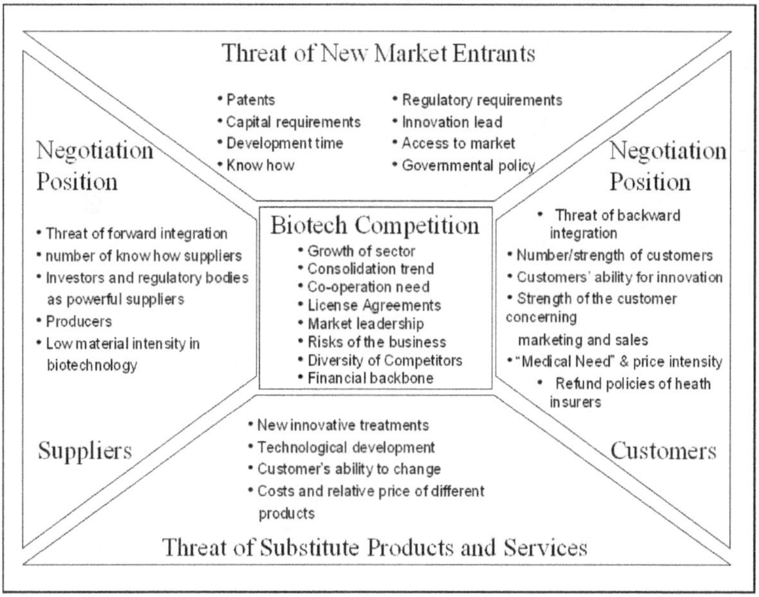

Figure 7: Application of Porter's 5 Forces Model in the Biotechnology Segment (Source: DVFA (2005), p. 50-51).

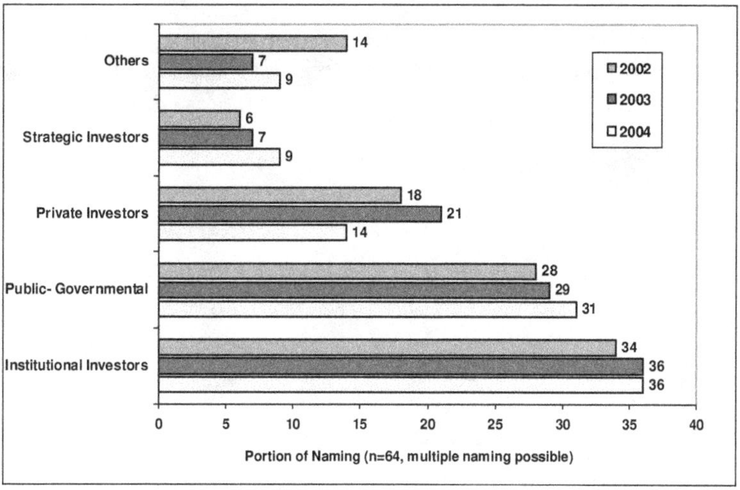

Figure 8: Capital Sources in Biotechnology according to an Ernst & Young Survey (Source: E&Y (2005), p. 97).

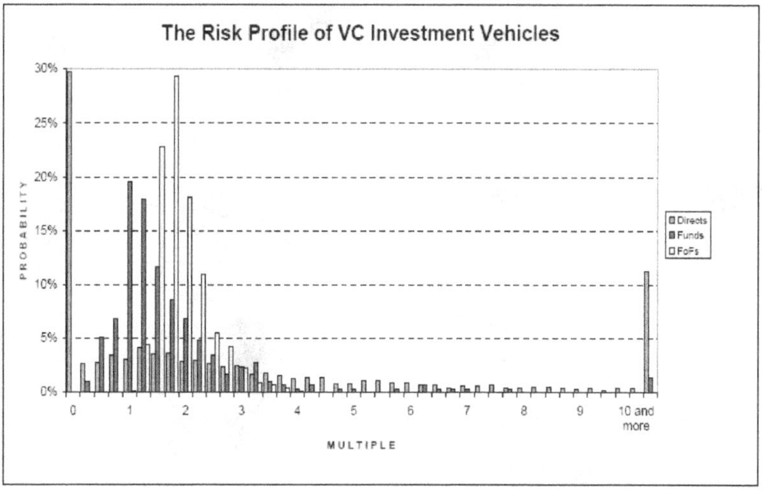

Figure 9:The Risk Profile of Venture Capital Investment Vehicles in the US

(Source: Weidig/Mathonet (2004), p. 28).

CPSIA information can be obtained
at www.ICGtesting.com
Printed in the USA
BVHW031201090322
631010BV00005B/147